BITCH!

edited by Jasmine Birtles

introduced by Kathy Lette

MICHAEL O'MARA BOOKS LIMITED

I'm tough, ambitious and I know what I want.
If that makes me a bitch, okay.

Madonna

First published as *Bitch!* in 1999 by Michael O'Mara Books Limited.
Previously published as *Women on Men and other laughing matters*
in 1994, also by Michael O'Mara Books Limited, 9 Lion Yard,
Tremadoc Road, London SW4 7NQ

A CIP catalogue record for this book is available from
the British Library

ISBN 1-85479-453-1

1 3 5 7 9 1 0 8 6 4 2

Designed and typeset by Keystroke,
Jacaranda Lodge, Wolverhampton
Printed and bound in Great Britain
by Cox & Wyman Ltd, Reading, Berks

CONTENTS

I DON'T THINK THAT'S VERY FUNNY

I get everything: colds, cockroaches, Born Again Christian leaflets, parking tickets, prank calls, free bowel-cancer testing kits, seaweed-kelp recipe chain letters, rare Asian, Hong Kong and Mongolian influenzas . . . The only thing I don't get are Blokes Jokes.

At parties, lowering my resistance with alcohol, I expose myself to the more contagious Irish and lightbulb strains. I get so paranoid about the approaching punchline that I invariably miss it. My body tenses as I sense that laughline coming . . . building up momentum like an express train. My face starts to spasm as it comes closer and closer . . . . Guffawing loudly, I baulk, hurling myself off my listener's platform. The joke's derailed and the waiting passengers frown down at my twitching remains . . . Oops. A bit early. (Believe me, derail a bloke's joke and the term 'punchline' takes on a whole new meaning.)

Being honest about my humour-ectomy doesn't improve things. I am constantly whisking the smile off a room full of male faces with lines like 'Oh, and then what happened?' or 'Is that it?' or 'Could you please explain that bit about the hunchbacked Mexican's homosexual Rottweiler?' Tired of being the odd ball out,

I occasionally twitter and splutter and clutch my sides for the entire duration of a joke, sobering up suddenly at the end and asking the reparteeist what he's been up to lately . . . Very reparteedious.

Needless to say, the reason I don't get blokes' jokes is because I'm female. And women aren't funny. I know that because men are constantly telling me so.

Of course there's been the odd fluke: Mae West, Dorothy Parker, Jilly Cooper, Sophie Tucker, Lily Tomlin, Bette Midler, Jennifer Saunders, Roseanne Arnold, Dawn French, Victoria Wood, Ruby Wax, Rita Rudner, Joan Rivers, Carol Burnett, Lucille Ball, Erma Bombeck, Jo Brand, Joyce Grenfell, Gracie Fields, Phyllis Diller, Whoopi Goldberg, Miriam Margoyles, Mary Tyler Moore, Maryanne Fahye, Jean Kitson, Julie Walters, Sue Townsend . . . but as Mother Nature is female – and as we all know, 'whim' is the plural of woman – there is always the odd exception to the rule.

The facts, as men keep telling me, are that women just don't go straight for the jocular vein.

. . . Oh, we do tell some jokes: Why did God invent men? Because dildoes can't take out the garbage. Why are women so bad at maths? Because they're always being told that 3 inches equals 10 inches. How do you get rid of cockroaches? Tell them you want a long-term relationship. Why did the Aussie bloke cross the road? Cause his dick was in the chicken. Did you hear about the miracle baby? It was born with a penis *and* a brain . . . But the trouble is, even if we know jokes, we just can't *tell* them.

I was at a dinner party recently where the men, ignoring the carefully interwoven seating plan, craned around their female companions in a boisterous barter-ing of 'Have you heard the one about?' Elbowing her way into this conversational scrum, one of the female guests finally got up the nerve to share something which had given her a bad attack of the 'ha-ha's; a promotional sign outside a Wooloomooloo Health Club which read, 'Fat and Ugly? . . . Want to just be ugly?' While the other women present impaled them-selves on their swizzle sticks with mirth, their male partners swapped bewildered glances. 'You see?' shrugged her hubby, puncturing our pleasure, 'women just aren't funny'. A perfect instance of a woman not telling a joke — because she married one.

One of the greatest differences between the sexes (and there are many, believe me. Do you know any female who waits for the Toilet Fairy to change the roll on the spindle? Have you ever seen a woman mime a Jimi Hendrix guitar solo: jump up, mid-stroll, to touch an overhanging branch; fiddle with the fridge thermostat just for fun?) is our sense of humour. The men I know don't seem to tell jokes so much as detonate them; firing off rounds of wisecracks: black belt masters in the art of tongue-fu. Whereas for my women friends, humour is more confessional, cathartic, self-deprecating. The highlight of a Girls Night Out is not the pelvic gyrations of some jock-strapped hunk of spunk, but stripping off to our emotional undies: a psychological striptease which reveals all.

Another difference is the level of aggression. I grew up in Australia on a diet of blokes' jokes: Why do women have cunts? So that men will talk to them. What's the definition of a woman? Something to lie down on while you're having a fuck. Why does a woman have two holes? So you can turn her upside down and carry her like a six-pack. What do you call an anorexic woman with thrush? A quarter-pounder with cheese. What's the hardest thing about a sex-change operation? Sewing in the anchovy. Why shouldn't women surf? It's so hard to get the smell out of the fish. On and on they go about how bad we smell and how bad we taste . . . Now sperm does not exactly taste like zabaglione . . . but do we make jokes about it?

These are merely my observations based on nothing but prejudice, personal experience and the desperate need to fill six pages of introduction. But what do the experts say? Scientists tell us that laughter is innate; it originates in the oldest part of the brain, the hypothalamus. Biologists maintain that laughter increases our biological fitness. Anthropologists have revealed that the Eskimos hold laughing competitions and women, in all cultures, laugh more often than men, especially in all-female groups. Why?

In truth, some people are funny and others have funniness thrust upon them. As the butt of God's biological joke, for the female of the species it's probably a case of laugh or die. First off, there's menstruation. Oh, the joy of turning thirteen to discover you'll be taken hostage by your hormones once a month. You've only just got used to this injustice when you realize that there actually is something worse than getting your period. Not getting it.

The Pudding Club holds new horrors: turning, overnight, into a nurse in a Benny Hill sketch with breasts arriving at least five minutes before you do and ankles so swollen that in the nude it looks as though you're wearing flesh-coloured flares. These symptoms pale when compared to the birth itself. To simulate the birth experience, take one car jack, insert into rectum, pump to maximum height and replace with jack hammer. And that would be a good birth. Not to mention the episiotomies, hysterectomies, mastitis, mastectomies, misogynistic men . . .

My first boyfriend, a surfer from Cronulla, used to get me to cut his name out in paper and sticky-tape it to my abdomen so that I would get a tan-tattoo in the shape of his name. I realized recently that if I ever get cancer the melanoma is going to be in the shape of 'Bruce'. Can you imagine it? A melanoma called Bruce. I'm going to have a Bruce-ectomy to kill it. Then I truly will be able to say, 'Laugh? **I nearly died.**'

Of course, one of the reasons men don't want to admit that women might be funny, is because they're terrified to think what it is we might be being funny about. Boys, to put you at ease, let me just say that at our all-girl gatherings, we don't just talk about length . . . We also talk about width. But mostly we just sit around being HFs (Humourless Feminists). Speaking of which, how many feminists does it take to tell a joke? Two. One to make the joke and the other to say, 'I don't think that's very funny.'

WOMEN ON MEN

Once a woman is made man's equal she
becomes his superior.

Margaret Thatcher

On the whole barristers are more
interested in their briefs than in a girl's.

Jilly Cooper, *Men and Super Men*

I only like two kinds of men: domestic and foreign.

Mae West

God made men stronger but not necessarily more intelligent. He gave women intuition and femininity and, used properly, that combination easily jumbles the brain of any man I ever met.

Farrah Fawcett

I think men are very funny. If I had one of those dangly things stuffed down the front of my pants, I'd sit at home all day laughing at myself.

Dawn French

The more I see of men the better I like
dogs.

Madame Roland (1754–93)

Nothing is more debasing for a real man
than a plastic apron.

Raine, Comtesse de Chambrun

There is a moment when a man develops enough confidence and ease in a relationship to bore you to death.

Eve Babitz

Blessed is the man who, having nothing to say, abstains from giving in words evidence of the fact.

George Eliot

Whenever I date a guy I think, is this the man I want my children to spend their weekends with?

Rita Rudner, comedienne

I'd need a lobotomy to be equal to a man in Hollywood.

Roseanne Arnold

A fox is a wolf who sends flowers.

Ruth Weston, actress

There is a vast difference between the savage and the civilized man, but it is never apparent to their wives until after breakfast.

Helen Rowland

Men are very simple creatures. Emotionally they are blockheads.

Irma Kurtz

It is quite difficult enough to trust oneself without trusting a man!

Elinor Glyn

He's the kind of bore who's here today and here tomorrow.

Binnie Barnes

Men are emotional bonsai. You have to whack the fertilizer on to get any feelings out of them.

Kathy Lette

The first time you buy a house you see how pretty the paint is and you buy it. The second time you look to see if the basement has termites. It's the same with men.

Lupe Velez, Mexican actress

Men are those creatures with two legs and eight hands.

Jayne Mansfield

There are only two kinds of men – the dead and the deadly.

Helen Rowland

Giving a man space is like giving a dog a computer: the chances are he will not use it nicely.

Bette-Jane Raphael

Men don't know anything about pain; they've never experienced labour, cramps or a bikini wax.

Nan Tisdale

No man has ever stuck his hand up your
dress looking for a library card.

Joan Rivers

With a head like yours, I am surprised you
don't get it circumcised.

**Pamela Armstrong to another debater in a
Cambridge Union debate**

Our Mothers always told us that one day
we would meet our Mr Rights . . . mind you,
they told us not to swim when we had our
periods.

Kathy Lette

Male heckler: 'Are you a lesbian?'
'Are you my alternative?'

Florence Kennedy

Men only call themselves feminists in the
hope of getting a more intelligent fuck.

Kathy Lette

If somebody makes me laugh, I'm his slave for life.

Bette Midler

When he's late for dinner, I know he's either having an affair or is lying dead in the street. I always hope it's the street.

Jessica Tandy

The only time a woman really succeeds in changing a man is when he's a baby.

Natalie Wood

It's not the men in my life, it's the life in my men.

Mae West

One of my theories is that men love with their eyes; women love with their ears.

Zsa Zsa Gabor

Men are taught to apologize for their weaknesses, women for their strengths.

Lois Wyse

You can seduce a man without taking
anything off, without even touching him.

Rae Dawn Chong

In passing, I would like to say that the first
time Adam had a chance he laid the blame
on woman.

Nancy, Lady Astor

Men say they love independence in a
woman, but they don't waste a second
demolishing it brick by brick.

Candice Bergen

Billing minus cooing.

Mary Dorsey, on alimony

Women speak because they wish to speak, whereas a man speaks only when driven to speech by something outside himself – like, for instance, he can't find any clean socks.

Jean Kerr

Once I went out with this guy who asked me to mother him – so I spat on a hanky and wiped his face.

Jenny Jones, US comedienne

A hard man's good to find – but you'll
mostly find him asleep.

Mae West

Some of my best leading men have been
horses and dogs.

Elizabeth Taylor

How do I feel about men? With my fingers.

Cher

Women prefer men who have something tender about them – especially the legal kind.

Kay Ingram

The fantasy of every Australian man is to have two women – one cleaning and the other dusting.

Maureen Murphy

Man invented language to satisfy his need to complain.

Lily Tomlin

WOMEN ON SEX

'Sex,' she says, 'is a subject like any other subject. Every bit as interesting as agriculture.'

Muriel Spark, novelist

I am the twentieth-century failure, a happy undersexed celibate.

Denise Coffey, comedienne

I had a good eight inches last night.

Ulrika Johnsson

He said, 'If I'd've known you were a virgin I'd've taken more time.'

I said, 'If I'd've known you had more time I'd've taken my tights off.'

Ellie Laine

The grass is always greener on the other side of the fence. So if you don't want to stain your skirt, do it on this side.

Joan Rivers

If sex is such a natural phenomenon, how come there are so many books on how to?

Bette Midler

Why women shouldn't give blow-jobs. Because its really off-putting seeing a man look that pathetically grateful, and you don't know how fattening it is.

Jenny Eclair

You know the worst thing about oral sex?
The view.

Maureen Lipman

Last night I asked my husband, 'What's your
favourite sexual position?' and he replied,
'Next door.'

Joan Rivers

If I was the Virgin Mary, I would have said no.

Stevie Smith, poet

Don't you hate it when your best male platonic friend ends up sleeping in your bed wearing just his pants and promises you nothing's gonna happen – and nothing does?

Charmian Hughes, comedienne

My message to the businessmen of this country when they go abroad on business is that there is one thing above all they can take with them to stop them catching AIDS, and that is the wife.

Edwina Currie, politician

You remember your first mountain in much the same way you remember having your first sexual experience, except that climbing doesn't make as much mess and you don't cry for a week if Ben Nevis forgets to phone the next morning.

Muriel Gray, TV presenter and writer

I've tried several varieties of sex. The conventional position makes me claustrophobic. And the others either give me a stiff neck or lockjaw.

Tallulah Bankhead

It's not sex that gives the pleasure, but the lover.

Marge Piercy

Absence does not make the heart grow fonder, but it sure heats up the blood.

Elizabeth Ashley

You mustn't force sex to do the work of love or love to do the work of sex.

Mary McCarthy

Shared laughter is erotic too.

Marge Piercy

All really great lovers are articulate, and verbal seduction is the surest road to actual seduction.

Marya Mannes

To err is human – but it feels divine.

Mae West

Sex is hardly ever just about sex.

Shirley MacLaine

The most important thing in acting is to be able to laugh and cry. If I have to cry, I think of my sex life. If I have to laugh, I think of my sex life.

Glenda Jackson

Conventional sexual intercourse is like squirting jam into a doughnut.

Germaine Greer

I see – she's the original good time that was had by all.

Bette Davis, referring to a starlet of the time

After lovemaking, do you,
   a) go to sleep?
   b) light a cigarette?
   c) return to the front of the bus?

Joan Rivers

WOMEN ON WOMEN

She must not swing her arms as though she were dangling ropes; she must not switch herself this way and that; she must not shout; and she must not, while wearing her bridal veil, smoke a cigarette.

Emily Post

Lesbianism has always seemed to me an extremely inventive response to the shortage of men but otherwise not worth the trouble.

Nora Ephron

The problem with some women is that they get all excited about nothing – and then they marry him.

Cher

Behind almost every woman you ever heard of stands a man who let her down.

Naomi Bliven, American writer

A lady is someone who never shows her underwear unintentionally.

Lillian Day, American writer

Smart girls know how to play tennis, piano and dumb.

Lynn Redgrave

Women are one of the Almighty's enigmas to prove to men that he knows more than they do.

Ellen Glasgow

I'm not denyin' the women are foolish:
God Almighty made 'em to match the men.

George Eliot

Whatever they try and sell you, the best
aphrodisiac for women is eating oysters
because if you can swallow oysters, you
can swallow anything.

Hattie Hayridge, comedienne

Being a woman is of special interest only to aspiring male transsexuals. To actual women, it is simply a good excuse not to play football.

Fran Lebowitz

I'm the intelligent, independent-type woman. In other words, a girl who can't get a man.

Shelley Winters, American actress

It's the good girls who keep their diaries; the bad girls never have the time.

Tallulah Bankhead

What you eat standing up doesn't count.

Beth Barnes

It's time to stop denying the 'inner bitch' in ourselves. Stop apologizing for her. Set her free.

Elizabeth Hilts

A woman is like a teabag. You never know how strong she is until she gets into hot water.

Eleanor Roosevelt

Big women are sexier – we pump more oestrogen, have higher sex drives and fantasize more.

Dawn French

If a few lustful and erotic reveries make the housework go by 'as if in a dream', why not?

Nancy Friday

Whatever women do they must do twice as well as men to be thought half as good. Luckily this is not difficult.

Charlotte Whitton

Plain women know more about men than beautiful ones do.

Katharine Hepburn

Women are taught that, to appear to yield is the only way to govern.

Sarah Moore Grimke

A woman without a man is like a fish without a bicycle.

Gloria Steinem

There is no female mind. The brain is not an organ of sex. Might as well speak of a female liver.

Charlotte Perkins Gilman

There are two kinds of women: those who want power in the world and those who want power in bed.

Jacqueline Kennedy Onassis

After an acquaintance of ten minutes many women will exchange confidences that a man would not reveal to a lifelong friend.

Page Smith

When a man gives his opinion he's a man.
When a woman gives her opinion she's a
bitch.

Bette Davis

Men have power and a power complex;
women just have a complex.

Yvonne Roberts

The most indolent women have been seen
running to catch a boss.

Jilly Cooper, *Men and Super Men*

Girls have got balls. They're just a little higher up, that's all.

Joan Jett, American rock singer

A girl can wait for the right man to come along, but in the meantime, that still doesn't mean she can't have a wonderful time with all the wrong ones.

Cher

A woman must have money and a room of her own.

Virginia Woolf

Both men and women are fallible. The difference is, women know it.

Eleanor Bron

Were women *meant* to do everything – work and have babies?

Candice Bergen

People call me a feminist whenever I express sentiments that differentiate me from a doormat or a prostitute.

Rebecca West

WOMEN ON LOVE AND MARRIAGE

Computer dating: it's terrific if you're a computer.

Rita Mae Brown

I thought *coq au vin* was love in a lorry.

Victoria Wood, *Talent*

A husband is what is left of a man after the
nerve is extracted.

Helen Rowland

What to wear in bed: something warm,
usually my husband.

Edwina Currie, politician

It seems to me that the desire to get
married – which, I regret to say, I believe
is basic and primal in women – is followed
almost immediately by an equally basic and
primal urge – which is to be single again.

Nora Ephron

When you see what some girls marry, you realize how they must hate to work for a living.

Helen Rowland

All girlfriends are like bluebottles. Some are just a bit harder to swat.

Jane Clark, wife of philandering Alan Clark

I married beneath me. All women do.

Nancy, Lady Astor

Getting divorced just because you don't love a man is almost as silly as getting married just because you do.

Zsa Zsa Gabor

Not all women give most of their waking thoughts to the problem of pleasing men. Some are married.

Emma Lee

Bigamy is when you're married to one man too many.

Monogamy is the same thing.

Erica Jong

At every party there are two kinds of people – those who want to stay and those who don't. The trouble is, they are usually married to each other.

Ann Landers

It should be a very happy marriage – they are both so much in love with him.

Irene Thomas, British broadcaster

I want a man who's kind and understanding. Is that too much to ask of a millionaire?

Zsa Zsa Gabor

One wishes marriage for one's daughter and, for one's descendants, better luck.

Fay Weldon, novelist

Hollywood is the only place in the world where amicable divorce means each one gets fifty per cent of the publicity.

Lauren Bacall

Love is or it ain't. Thin love ain't love at all.

Toni Morrison

I am a marvellous housekeeper. Every time
I leave a man I keep his home.

Zsa Zsa Gabor

A woman scorned is a woman who quickly
learns her way around a courtroom.

Colette Mann

There is so little between husbands, you
might as well keep the first.

Adela Rogers St John

I sometimes think that being widowed is
God's way of telling you to come off the Pill.

Victoria Wood, *Barmy*

My mother said it was simple to keep a
man, you must be a maid in the living room,
a cook in the kitchen and a whore in the
bedroom. I said I'd hire the first two and
take care of the bedroom bit.

Jerry Hall

An archaeologist is the best husband any woman can have: the older she gets, the more interested he is in her.

Agatha Christie

The loss of first love is so painful that it borders on the ludicrous.

Maya Angelou

Some of my colleagues are so keen on family values that they choose to have more than one of them.

Edwina Currie, politician

In love there are two things: bodies and words.

Joyce Carol Oates

People keep asking me if I'll marry again. It's as if after you've had one car crash you want another.

Stephanie Beacham

Love is the extremely difficult realization that something other than oneself is real.

Iris Murdoch

Opposites attract, but like is much easier to be married to.

Diana Douglas Darrid

It is a curious thought, but it is only when you see people looking ridiculous, that you realize how much you love them.

Agatha Christie

If only one could tell true love from false love as one can tell mushrooms from toadstools.

Katherine Mansfield

A married couple is a dangerous machine!

Iris Murdoch

Ideally couples need three lives: one for him, one for her and one for them together.

Jacqueline Bisset

Age does not protect you from love. But love, to some extent, protects you from age.

Jeanne Moreau

The hardest task in a girl's life is to prove
to a man that his intentions are serious.

Helen Rowland

Love involves a peculiar unfathomable
combination of understanding and misunder-
standing.

Diane Arbus

Marrying a man is like buying something
you've been admiring for a long time in
a shop window. You may love it when you
get it home, but it doesn't always go with
everything.

Jean Kerr

The Eskimo has fifty-two names for snow
because it is important to them; there ought
to be as many for love.

Margaret Atwood

I hope the dress brings someone more
happiness than it brought me. On our
wedding day, Marco said he didn't like it.

**Lisa Butcher, Marco Pierre White's ex-wife, on
donating her wedding dress to a charity raffle**

Love is a fire. But whether it is going to warm your hearth or burn down your house, you can never tell.

Joan Crawford

Anyone who's a great kisser I'm interested in.

Cher

A man should kiss his wife's navel every day.

Nell Kimball

WOMEN ON LOVE AND MARRIAGE

Did you read about the woman who
stabbed her husband thirty-seven times?
I admire her restraint.

Roseanne Arnold

Sex is an emotion in motion ... Love is what
you make it and who you make it with.

Mae West

Husbands are like fires. They go out when
unattended.

Zsa Zsa Gabor

One of the oldest human needs is having someone to wonder where you are when you don't come home at night.

Margaret Mead

A man is designed to walk three miles in the rain to phone for help when the car breaks down. And the woman is designed to say 'You took your time' when the man comes back dripping wet.

Victoria Wood

WOMEN ON PRIDE

I think Mick Jagger would be astounded and amazed if he realized how to many people he is not a sex symbol.

Angie Bowie

The best fame is a writer's fame: it's enough to get a table at a good restaurant, but not enough that you get interrupted when you eat.

Fran Lebowitz

Honey, I don't care what they call me, as long as they don't quit talking about me.

Bette Midler

I have to be seen to be believed.

The Queen

I've never had a humble opinion. If you've got an opinion, why be humble about it?

Joan Baez

He claims to be great sexual athlete, just because he always comes first.

Ellie Laine

I've been on a calendar, but never on time.

Marilyn Monroe

Don't be humble. You're not that great.

Golda Meir

I don't care what is written about me so
long as it isn't true.

Dorothy Parker

Being in love with yourself means never
having to say you've got a headache.

Ellie Laine

WOMEN ON MOTHERHOOD AND GROWING UP

Next time I'm not just having an epidural for the birth – I'm having one for the conception as well.

Sally James

If men had to have babies, they would only ever have one.

Diana, Princess of Wales

Natural Birth: a case of stiff upper labia.

Kathy Lette

You can't drink and smoke because it would retard the baby's growth. Actually that's a good idea because then they'd just fall out and you could just dress them in an old sock.

Jenny Eclair

Mrs Hall of Sherbourne was brought to
bed yesterday of a dead child, some weeks
before she expected, owing to a fright. I
suppose she happened unawares to look
at her husband.

Jane Austen, 1798

I'm at that stage of motherhood where I'm
putting the kids under the sink and the lethal
household substances within reach.

Kathy Lette

Do you think those triplets were really mine? After all, I did only go into hospital to have my ears pierced.

Victoria Wood, *Barmy*

The English hate children. They keep their dogs at home and send their kids off to high-class kennels, called Eton and Harrow.

Kathy Lette

People who say they sleep like babies usually don't have one.

Moyra Bremner

Having a baby boy is where feminist theory collides into reality with a juddering crash.

Dianne Abbott, politician

Let's face it, if God had meant men to have children, he would have given them PVC aprons.

Victoria Wood, *Up to You, Porky*

I knew I was an unwanted child when I saw
that my bath toys were a toaster and a
radio.

Joan Rivers

The moment you have children yourself, you
forgive your parents everything.

Susan Hill, novelist

If you want your children to listen, try talking
softly – to someone else.

Ann Landers

Any mother could perform the jobs of several air-traffic controllers with ease.

Lisa Alther

Is nothing in life ever straight and clear, the way children see it?

Rosie Thomas

Never lend your car to anyone to whom you have given birth.

Erma Bombeck

Remember that as a teenager you are at the last stage in your life when you will be happy to hear that the phone is for you.

Fran Lebowitz

There's a lot more to being a woman than being a mother, but there's a hell of a lot more to being a mother than most people suspect.

Roseanne Arnold

Women who miscalculate are called mothers.

Abigail van Buren

It goes without saying that you should never have more children than you have car windows.

Erma Bombeck

The real menace in dealing with a five-year-old is that in no time at all you begin to sound like a five-year-old.

Jean Kerr

I used to think it was a pity that her mother rather than she had not thought of birth control.

Muriel Spark, on Dr Marie Stopes

The best thing that could happen to motherhood already has. Fewer women are going into it.

Victoria Billings

In Australia, breeding is something we do with dogs.

Kathy Lette

WOMEN ON FIRST IMPRESSIONS

Whenever my mother sees me she says,
'Jenny, Jenny, why aren't you wearing a
petticoat?'
'Mother, it's because I've got jeans on.'

Jenny Eclair

Dress code is everything. You can be a card-
carrying Nazi, or pay gigolos to eat gnocchi
out of your navel, and you won't be pilloried.
But never, ever wear linen with tweed.

Kathy Lette

I base most of my fashion taste on what doesn't itch.

Gilda Radner

Pardon my long preamble. It's like a chorus girl's tights – it touches everything and covers nothing.

Gertrude Lawrence, in an after-dinner speech

It's an ill-wind that blows when you leave the hairdresser.

Phyllis Diller

I'm tired of all this nonsense about beauty
being only skin deep. That's deep enough.
What do you want – an adorable pancreas?

Jean Kerr

It doesn't matter to me that you haven't
seen your navel in twenty-five years and that
you can wear your stomach as a kilt. Tell me
you're happy.

Jennifer Saunders, *Absolutely Fabulous*

Women dress alike all over the world: they dress to be annoying to other women.

Elsa Schiaparelli, Italian couturière

I was on a beach last summer, on a lovely beach sunbathing, and one of those life-guards came up and he said to me, 'Madam, you'll have to move – the tide wants to come in.'

Marjorie Rea, comedienne

Hats divide generally into three classes:
offensive hats, defensive hats and shrapnel.

Katherine Whitehorn

I wanted the bags under my eyes unpacking.
They looked as if they were ready for a
round-the-world cruise.

Liz Dawn, actress

If I hadn't had them, I would have had some
made.

Dolly Parton, on her most obvious assets

The reason there are so few female politicians is that it is too much trouble to put make-up on two faces.

Maureen Murphy, politician

Edina: What you don't realize is that inside, inside of me there is a thin person just screaming to get out.
Mother: Just the one, dear?

Jennifer Saunders, *Absolutely Fabulous*

WOMEN ON PERSONALITIES

Patsy: Shahpari Kashoggi . . . All that money and she's still got a moustache . . . Look, darling, one more face-lift and she'd have a beard.

Jennifer Saunders, *Absolutely Fabulous*

When I appear in public people expect me
to neigh, grind my teeth, paw the ground
and swish my tail – none of which is easy.

Princess Anne

Sir Stafford has a brilliant mind, until it is
made up.

Margot Asquith, on Sir Stafford Cripps

The chopper has changed my life as
conclusively as that of Anne Boleyn.

Queen Elizabeth, the Queen Mother

I, along with the critics, have never taken myself very seriously.

Elizabeth Taylor

Better than cystitis.

Jo Brand's suggested slogan to boost John Major's popularity

The censors wouldn't even let me sit on a guy's lap, and I've been on more laps than a table napkin.

Mae West

My whole career has been an act of revenge.

Ruby Wax

Most Conservatives believe a crèche is something that happens between two Range Rovers in Tunbridge Wells.

Caroline Shorten, politician

Some people spend their lives failing and never notice.

Judith Rossner, American novelist

The trouble with being a princess is that it is so hard to have a pee.

Diana, Princess of Wales

Unfortunately, sometimes people don't hear you until you scream.

Stefanie Powers

I stopped believing in Santa Claus when I was six. Mother took me to see him in a department store, and he asked for my autograph.

Shirley Temple

I used to be snow-white until I drifted.

Mae West

When people ask me why I am running as a woman, I always answer, 'What choice do I have?'

Patricia Schroeder, Congresswoman

I'm tough, ambitious and I know what I want.
If that makes me a bitch, okay.

Madonna

I suppose I could have stayed home and
baked cookies and had teas.

Hillary Clinton

I always tell film-makers I'm happy to run
around in the buff if the co-star runs around
with his willy hanging out.

Michelle Pfeiffer

Success for me is having ten honeydew melons and eating only the top half of each one.

Barbra Streisand

I've made so many movies playing a hooker that they don't pay me in the regular way any more. They leave it on the dresser.

Shirley MacLaine

I don't want to be a passenger in my own life.

Diane Ackerman

Lead me not into temptation; I can find the way myself.

Rita Mae Brown

WOMEN ON AGE

The older one grows, the more one likes indecency.

Virginia Woolf

If I had any decency, I'd be dead. Most of my friends are.

Dorothy Parker, aged seventy

I refuse to admit that I'm more than fifty-two, even if that does make my sons illegitimate.

Nancy, Lady Astor

The secret of staying young is to live honestly, eat slowly and lie about your age.

Lucille Ball

Edina: If my mother hadn't uncrossed her legs so early I'd have been two weeks younger.

Jennifer Saunders, *Absolutely Fabulous*

A woman is as young as her knee.

Mary Quant

Take a close-up of a woman past sixty! You might as well use a picture of a relief map of Ireland!

Nancy, Lady Astor

I was born in 1962, true. And the room next to me was 1963.

Joan Rivers

I have everything I had twenty years ago, only it's all a little bit lower.

Gypsy Rose Lee

I wonder if I should get some hormone replacement packs here in the house for emergencies. One day you might come home and find a toothless wad of old gum on the floor and have to slap some glands on.

Jennifer Saunders, *Absolutely Fabulous*

I believe the second half of one's life is meant to be better than the first half. The first half is finding out how to do it. And the second half is enjoying it.

Frances Lear

If we don't change, we don't grow. If we don't grow, we are not really living.

Gail Sheehy

Old age is like a plane flying through a storm. Once you're aboard, there's nothing you can do.

Golda Meir

Age is something that doesn't matter unless you are a cheese.

Billie Burke

One of the many things nobody ever tells you about middle age is that it's such a nice change from being young.

Dorothy Canfield Fisher

It's sad to grow old, but nice to ripen.

Brigitte Bardot

Nature gives you the face you have at twenty; it is up to you to merit the face you have at fifty.

Coco Chanel

I'm aiming by the time I'm fifty to stop being an adolescent.

Wendy Cope

People change and forget to tell each other.

Lillian Hellman

Memory is more indelible than ink.

Anita Loos

The only thing that makes life possible is permanent, intolerable uncertainty; not knowing what comes next.

Ursula LeGuin

Maturity: a Stoic response to endless reality.

Carrie Fisher

Old age ain't no place for sissies

Bette Davis

WOMEN ON VICE, MONEY AND GREED

Champagne: I drink it when I am happy and when I'm sad. Sometimes I drink it when I'm alone. When I have company I consider it obligatory. I trifle with it if I'm not hungry and drink it when I am. Otherwise I never touch it – unless I'm thirsty.

Madam Lily Bollinger

Never eat more than you can lift.

Miss Piggy

Reality is a crutch for people who can't cope with drugs.

Lily Tomlin

A diamond is the only kind of ice that keeps a girl warm.

Elizabeth Taylor

In the 1960s everybody took drugs to expand their consciousness. In the 1970s they took them to get rid of it.

Grace Slick, American rock singer

Doctors don't ask the right questions to find out whether you have a drink problem. They should ask things like, 'Have you ever woken up on a plane to Turkey?' 'Has Oliver Reed ever said to you, "Push off, mate, I'm going home now"?' That's a drink problem.

Jenny Lecoat, comedienne

I am not a glutton, I am an explorer of food.

Erma Bombeck

One more drink and I'll be under the host.

Dorothy Parker, commenting at a party

I tried not drinking once. I heard myself talking all night and then, worse than that, next day I had total recall. It was terrifying.

Jennifer Saunders, *Absolutely Fabulous*

The only thing I like about rich people is their money.

Nancy, Lady Astor

There's a really nothing wrong with a woman welcoming all men's advances, as long as they are in cash.

Zsa Zsa Gabor

A gold rush is what happens when a line of chorus girls spots a man with a bankroll.

Mae West

Why should we mind if men have their faces on the money, as long as we get our hands on it?

Ivy Baker Priest, US Government official

I'm promoting cigarettes as a reaction against puritanism because puritanism can seriously damage your health.

Vivienne Westwood

WOMEN ON WISDOM

Keep your talent in the dark and you'll never be insulted.

Elsa Maxwell

Too often, the opportunity knocks, but by the time you push back the chain, push back the bolt, unhook the two locks and shut off the burglar alarm, it's too late.

Rita Coolidge

Only time can heal your broken heart, just as time can heal his broken arms and legs.

Miss Piggy

Happiness is good health and a bad memory.

Ingrid Bergman

You can only sleep your way to the middle.

Dawn Steel, film producer

Time wounds all heels.

Jane Ace

The more flesh you show, the further up the ladder you go.

Kim Basinger

If I had my life to live again, I'd make the same mistakes, only sooner.

Tallulah Bankhead

If lawyers are disbarred and clergymen defrocked, doesn't it follow that electricians can be delighted; musicians denoted; cowboys deranged; models deposed; tree surgeons debarked and dry cleaners depressed?

Victoria Ostman

Outside every thin girl is a fat man trying to get in.

Katherine Whitehorn

The train which never seems to run late is the one on the timetable just before mine.

Caroline Balcon

Advice is what we ask for when we already know the answer but wish we didn't.

Erica Jong

Nagging is the repetition of unpalatable truths.

Edith Summerskill

As soon as life becomes bearable we stop analysing it . . . A tranquil day is spoiled by being examined.

George Sand

Find out what you like doing best and get someone to pay you for doing it.

Katherine Whitehorn

Time is the one thing with which all women should be miserly.

Agnes E Meyer

Show me a person who has never made a mistake and I'll show you somebody who has never achieved much.

Joan Collins

Some things are important and some are very unimportant. To know the difference is what we are given life to find out.

Anna F Trevisan

Never economize on luxuries.

Angela Thirkell

The most popular labour-saving device is still money.

Phyllis George

Sometimes it is less hard to wake up feeling lonely when you are alone than to wake up feeling lonely when you are with someone.

Liv Ullmann

There must be quite a few things a hot bath won't cure, but I don't know many of them.

Sylvia Path

I think the one lesson I have learned is that there is no substitute for paying attention.

Diane Sawyer

Reality is something you rise above.

Liza Minelli

There is no pleasure in having nothing to do;
the fun is in having lots to do and not doing
it.

Mary Little

The way I see it, if you want the rainbow,
you gotta put up with the rain.

Dolly Parton

Arrange whatever pieces come your way.

Virginia Woolf

Above all, remember that the most
important thing you can take anywhere is
not a Gucci bag or French-cut jeans; it's an
open mind.

Freda Adler

I do not know anyone who has got to the
top without hard work. That is the recipe.
It will not always get you to the top, but
should get you pretty near.

Margaret Thatcher

You can lead a whore to culture but you can't make her think.

Dorothy Parker

Woman's virtue is man's greatest invention.

Cornelia Otis Skinner, American actress

The first problem for all of us, men and women, is not to learn, but to unlearn.

Gloria Steinem

WOMEN ON MODERN LIVING

Life is too short to stuff a mushroom.

Shirley Conran, *Superwoman*

If you can keep your head when all about you are losing theirs, it's quite possible you haven't grasped the situation.

Jean Kerr

I worry about scientists discovering that lettuce has been fattening all along.

Erma Bombeck

Why do Born-Again people so often make you wish they'd never been born the first time?

Katherine Whitehorn

A car is useless in New York, essential everywhere else. The same with good manners.

Mignor McLaughlin

An occasional visit to a fast-food restaurant is not the worst of possible sins.

Hillary Clinton

Now that we all travel abroad so much, there comes a dreadful moment in our lives when our foreign friends, whom we strongly urged to visit us, actually do so.

Virginia Graham

I was in a cab the other day. The driver was going on and on about how Americans get into this weird violence. I wanted to knife the bastard.

Kit Hollerbach, American comedienne, in Britain

I wonder what the French say when they get déjà vu?

Hattie Hayridge, comedienne

People would have more leisure time if it weren't for all the leisure-time activities that use it up.

Peg Bracken

It hurt like hell, but it's still less painful than not eating.

Roseanne Arnold, on stomach-reduction surgery

If you would like more information on the full list of humour titles published by Michael O'Mara Books Limited please contact our UK sales department on:

Fax: 0171 622 6956

E-mail: humour@michaelomarabooks.com

Titles include:

- The Complete History of Farting
- The World's Greatest Lies
- On Second Thoughts
- Bitch!
- The Stupidest Things Ever Said
- The Stupidest Things Ever Done
- Stupid Sex
- The Nastiest Things Ever Said